MY MOMMY'S HANDS!

by Sunny Davis

illustrated by Penny Weber

To my Kelly
a wonderful daughter
and an exceptional mother

ISBN 979-8-9895977-0-3 (Hardcover)

ISBN 979-8-9895977-1-0 (Paperback)

Davis Literary

For permissions contact: davisliterary@gmail.com

It's morning time,
I'm glad to say;
Mommy's hands
will start my day!

Mommy gets me
out of bed
and plants a kiss
upon my head.

My bottom's wet
and has a smell.
Mommy's hands
will clean me well!

It's her love
that makes a way
to do this task
throughout each day.

Pajamas off -
It's time for clothes!
Mommy's hands
will help with those!

Very cute
and very fresh,
Mommy's why
I look my best!

I'm so hungry –
time to eat!
Mommy's hands
make me a treat!

In the morning,
eve, or day,
Mommy's food
is freshly made.

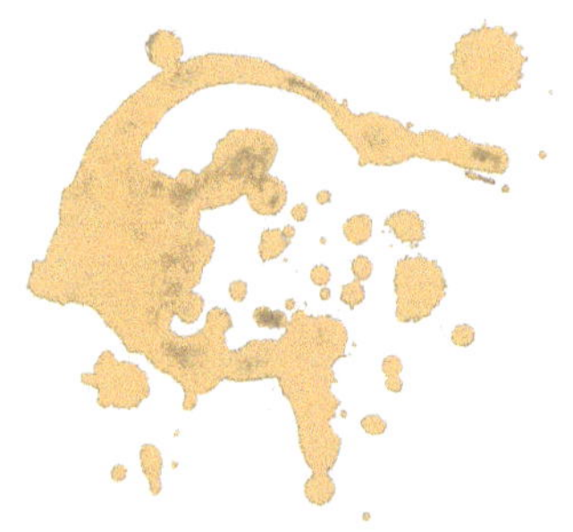

On my plate
or in my cup;
Mommy's food will
fill me up!

Eating's done;
I liked the taste!
Mommy's hands
will wipe my face!

If my food
is on the floor,
Mommy's hands
will clean some more!

Wiping crumbs
or milky foam,
Mommy keeps
a healthy home

To the park;
my favorite thing!
Mommy's hands
will push my swing!

Then she sits me
on the slide,
and holds me tight
while down I glide.

After nap,
we exercise!
Mommy's hands will
help me rise!

Curling, reaching,
stretching long,
Mommy makes
my body strong!

My small steps
are sometimes slow.
Mommy's hands
help me to go!

If I fall,
she's always here
to pick me up
and calm my fear.

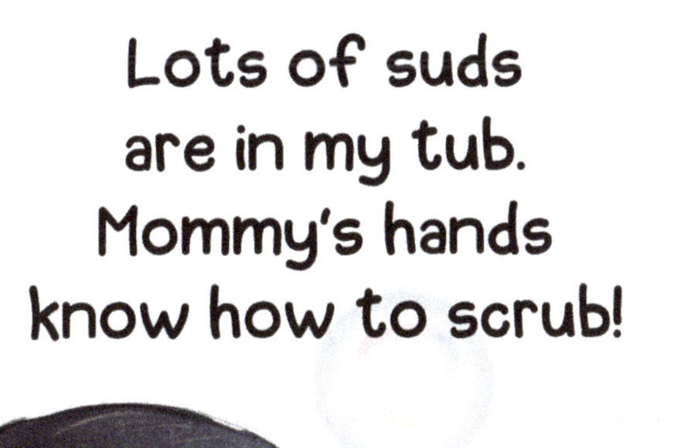

Lots of suds
are in my tub.
Mommy's hands
know how to scrub!

I will splash
and get her wet,
but she never
gets upset!

Story time
will end our day.
Mommy's hand
will turn each page.

With the book
in front of me,
pretty pictures
I can see.

It's time for bed;
I'm sleepy now!
Mommy's hands
will lay me down.

As I start
to fall asleep
Mommy's hands
will stroke my cheek

Mommy's

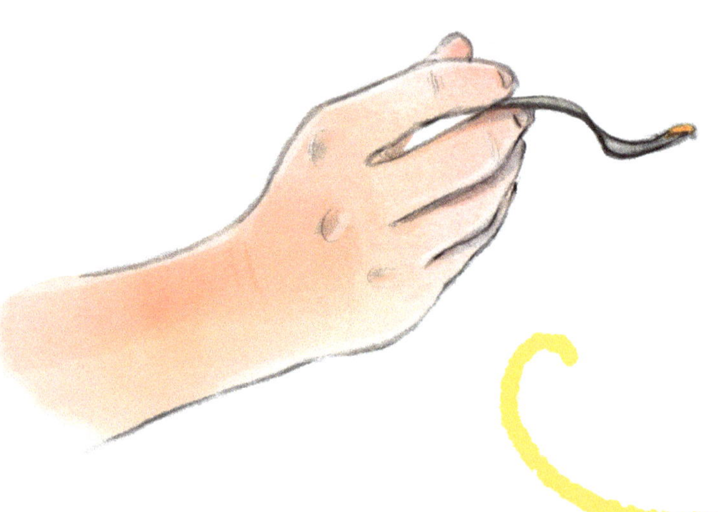

hands...

...are miracles!